510y

KU-020-140

Sorting

David Kirkby

First published in Great Britain by Heinemann Library
an imprint of Heinemann Publishers (Oxford) Ltd
Halley Court, Jordan Hill, Oxford OX2 8EJ

MADRID ATHENS PARIS
FLORENCE PRAGUE WARSAW
PORTSMOUTH NH CHICAGO SAO PAULO
SINGAPORE TOKYO MELBOURNE AUCKLAND
IBADAN GABERONE JOHANNESBURG

Designed by The Pinpoint Design Company
Printed in China

99 98 97 96 95
10 9 8 7 6 5 4 3 2 1

ISBN 0431 07955 2

British Library Cataloguing in Publication Data available on
request from the British Library.

Acknowledgements
The Publishers would like to thank the following
for the kind loan of equipment and materials
used in this book: Boswells, Oxford; The Early Learning
Centre; Lewis', Oxford; W. H. Smith; N. E. S. Arnold.
Special thanks to the children of St Francis C.E. First School

Photography: Chris Honeywell, Oxford

Cover photograph: Chris Honeywell, Oxford

Contents

The odd one out is different from all the others.

The ruler is the odd one out.
You cannot write with it.

Which one is the odd one out?

To do:
Copy these things
to eat.
Which is the
odd one out?

This is a block graph.

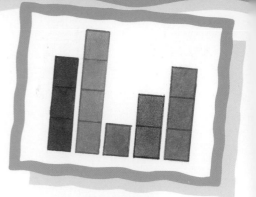

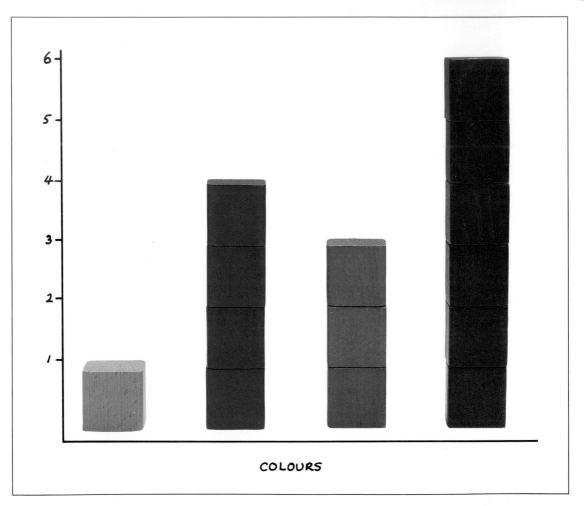

COLOURS

Count the blocks for each colour. This block graph shows us that red is the most popular colour.

6

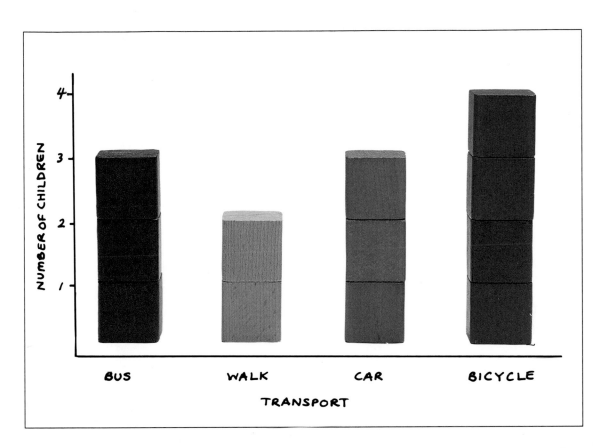

How many children travel by bus?
What else does the block graph
tell you?

To do:
Here are 10 children's
favourite colours.
Draw a block graph
to show this.

6 children blue
2 children yellow
1 child red
1 child green

This is a pictograph. It uses pictures or drawings.

SPRING

SUMMER

AUTUMN

WINTER

BOYS

GIRLS

This pictograph shows how many boys and girls there are in our team.

8

On which days did I eat exactly
2 slices of bread?

What else does the pictograph
tell you?

To do:
Draw a pictograph to
show how many apples
you eat in one week.

9

Tallies are used to keep count.
They are bunched in fives.

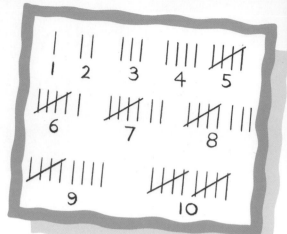

A dog is the most common pet.

Are the tallies correct?

To do:
Throw a dice 10 times.
Draw a tally chart to
show the results.

This is a bar graph.
These are the bars.

Swimming is the favourite sport,
then football.

How many children have green eyes?

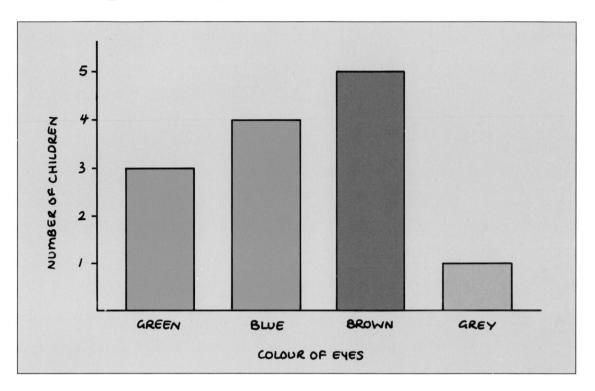

What else does this bar graph tell you?

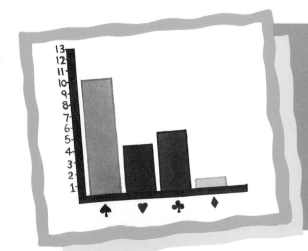

To do:
Deal out 20 playing cards.
Draw a bar graph to show how many cards of each suit there are.

13

A list helps you to remember things.

This is a shopping list.

Some things on this menu are in the wrong place.

MENU

Drinks
Milk Shakes
Tea
Orange juice
Roast chicken

Main Course
Ice cream
Fish pie
Pasta
Burger and chips

Dessert
Apple pie
Pizza
Chocolate cake

Can you put them in the right place?

TODAY'S JOBS

To do:
Make a list of things you need to do today.

15

In some card games you need to sort the cards.

These cards have been sorted into sets.

How have these cards been sorted?

To do:
Find a pack of playing cards.
Find different ways of sorting them.

A Venn diagram uses circles to sort things.

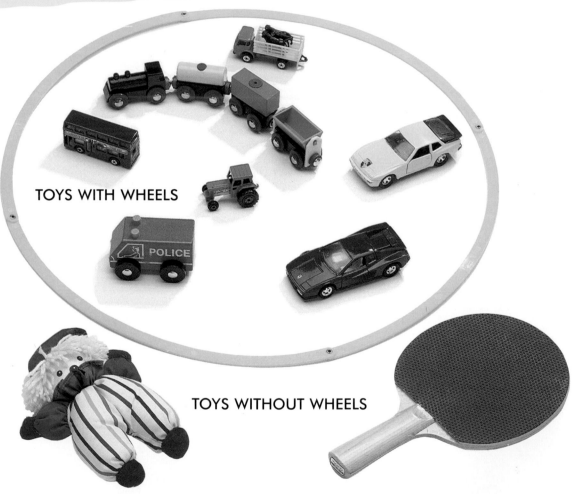

TOYS WITH WHEELS

TOYS WITHOUT WHEELS

These objects have been sorted inside and outside the circle.

STRAIGHT SIDES

CURVED SIDES

Where should the children put their shapes?

To do:
Where do these numbers go on this Venn diagram?

1
2
3
4
5

numbers more than 3

6
7
8
9
10

numbers less than 6

Sometimes we have to work out how things have been sorted.

Katy has sorted the biscuits.

How has the bread been sorted?

To do:
Here are 8 things you
can eat.
Sort them into 2
groups.

A survey helps us
to find things out.

Do you like Pizza?
☐ YES
☐ NO

What is your
favourite fruit?

In some surveys we vote.
Voting means choosing.

22

In some surveys we answer questions.

How many children have been surveyed here?

To do:
Do your own survey.
Find out some friends' favourite drink.

Favourite drinks
milk
lemonade
tea

answers

Page 5   Skipping rope. **To do:** Chocolate
Page 7   3 children travel by bus. 2 children walk.
          3 children travel by car. 4 children travel
          by bicycle
Page 9   On Tuesday and Sunday. Monday –
          4 slices, Wednesday and Saturday – 1 slice,
          Thursday – 5 slices, Friday – 3 slices
Page 11   Yes, the tallies are correct
Page 13   3 children have green eyes. 4 children have
          blue eyes. 5 children have brown eyes.
          1 child has grey eyes
Page 15   Roast chicken is a main course. Ice cream is
          a dessert. Pizza is a main course.
Page 17   Red odd numbers. Black even numbers.
          Numbers in order. Picture cards
Page 19   Red square goes in blue circle. Blue
          semi-circle goes in the middle (in both
          circles)
Page 21   The bread is sorted into loaves and rolls
Page 23   10 children

---

index